I Find You in the Darkness

poems

Alfa

Castle Point Books
New York

Contents

How many people have I lost

in my lifetime? I will never understand why the Universe planted me in an environment alongside people who were meant to be in my life forever, and then plucked them from my side. I've watched a stranger's face turn opal and heard his heart cease to beat in my unsuspecting arms. A body stays warm for a while after the spirit leaves its confines, *did you know that?* There is no life ebbing, just blue lips, and unbearable weight...but the skin holds on to *what once was*. I've felt souls leave rooms.... I watched them rise and dissipate. *Maybe that was my imagination—* but the air bends, and *life* leaves. There is always a void after a passing. A tear in normalcy. I try to recall their faces now, and as the years move on, so do the fine details. But sometimes...when I am alone, swathed in the quiet I seek, a movie reel will begin to slide left to right, before my eyes— and I see them, *one by one*. My heart beats with intention, reminding me that even after death, memories have their own pulse. Some more real than others. And I reach, because I have never fully let go. I reach, so I can find you in the darkness.

VESPER

Past holding

They tell me I'm weak

because *I hold on*

to my love for you.

But they do not know

the amount of strength required

in *never letting go*.

Windmill

You are encountering a heart that is returning home from war. It needs love—*but it needs understanding more.* It has seen things that may not make sense to you, or may not affect you in the same way...maybe these things would never have broken *you.* Loss is funny that way. Some people get through grieving gracefully, and go on to fill the emptiness with a new adventure. But this heart is a windmill, with love flowing round and round its center. It's not a gentle breeze that cascades slowly across a field of untouched wildflowers, but is a whirlwind that has been harnessed by the storage of suppressed storms. And this heart is trying to find a way to channel this power for *good.* Because it knows *that pain can be transformed into beauty,* if it is released in a way that helps someone else *get through* their own heartache.

Get to it

It seems like you have it all figured out.

Grieve.

Get through it.

And then *get to it*.

But what if my *get to it*

is merely to *get through* the *grieving*

—over and over again.

Death

We hold hands and tell each other how sorry we are. We endure. We comfort the only way we know how. We hold, we hug, we weep.

We *sing song* stories of *remember when…* recalling when a person was young and stood on bold legs, having had more days in front of them than behind them.

We play the highlight reel. We share pictures and stories. *We celebrate life when there is a death.* We give the person lying in the casket our undivided attention…the *time* we never gave them when they were alive.

Visitation

Everyone talks about Hell like they cannot wait to go. They throw that word around like it's on their bucket list.

Scratch it off.

I have been there and rode the flames since I hung up the phone and realized I would never see him again.

Check mark.

Just like you used to do

There is a place I go to when I want to
find you.

When I want to find the *best* of you.

The place we created, you and me.

I stoop in the garden and rub the dirt

between my fingers, testing for moisture.

Just like you used to do.

I look upward and ask Heaven for rain,

out of habit.

Just like you used to do.

And I ask you… to help me through this pain.

Just like you used to do.

Consoling

There are hands everywhere.

Arms wrapping me.

I'm in the crook of scented necks.

I'm chest to chest with people

that are blank faces and unknown to me.

Pats on backs, touching me, consoling me.

I watch your *life* walk past

the casket I have intentionally closed.

A 24 x 24 brazen self-portrait sits atop,

surrounded by white carnations you hated.

The people you interacted with daily

walk like zombies,

then turn to me.

They feel sorry for me.

Me.

*They act like I am the one lying in
that casket.*

Someone's forever

He wants to marry me and make me his.
Trepidation drips from my heart like it's
been submerged in an ocean filled with
other prospective souls.

And I ask him *why me. Why do you want to
marry me?* And he says something that
roots me to my spot and I cannot turn away.

He tells me he wants to wake up next to
me every morning. He wants me to be his—
forever.

*And I have always wanted to be
someone's forever.*

Hungry

I find myself not accepting trust as I grow older. I've learned that even people who are *deemed trustworthy* can stand two inches away from your lips, meet you eye to eye, and tell you what they *think* you want to hear. And oftentimes it is not the truth. They know *you're hungry for love* and for the feel-good moments that we all crave, and they are hand-feeding you crumbs of whatever it is they think whets your appetite. If only our hearts could tell us when they were truly full.

We'd never go back for seconds.

Selfish

The hardest part is this.

I was selfish.

I always thought you loved me,

much more than I loved you.

And now I know you did not.

Because I do not know if you loved me at all.

Player

It is always the same in the beginning.

You think they are different. A Prince.
A Knight in Shining Armor. A Viking.
They try hard to impress you, you know.
You will never know how many hours of
thought and test-runs went into the little
things he does to make himself stand out.
He's had a lot of practice. Remember all
those relationships…those ones he's told you
about, when he was misunderstood and
cheated on? If someone has a track record
that meanders around the park and has a
standing line down the block, *I behoove you
to tread lightly.* He is experienced at
playing the game. He tells you what he wants
you to hear. Is he a musician, by chance?
Because he is playing you like a fiddle in
need of a workout.

Enough

When I have a memory

like the one I had *roll through* today,

Sirens blaring,

forcing me to move my soul

to the side of the road...

I feel like I've had enough;

I'm flat.

Steamrolled into pavement.

I've had enough to last a lifetime.

Are you ready?

Are you ready to go through it again? I know the first few weeks are idyllic. It's always that way when taking back a *serial cheater* at the start. But you know it will wear off, right? Reality will settle in. You take him back, *thinking he will never do it again.* Do you really think that, or are you focusing on his 100 percent participation right now? Those promises have a way of stroking your inner soul. We always want the one who will fight for our heart...and my God, *he is fighting hard.* He is giving you more attention right this minute than he ever has, and you are hoping...*no, you are praying,* he means it this time. But a few weeks down the road when he takes a long lunch break, or seems distant, or doesn't come home right after work—if he is unaccounted for, for any length of time...*what is your mind going to do?* Be honest with yourself. Are you ready to go through it all over again?

Crescent moon

The world closes in. Too much light makes
me believe that I'm supposed to be here.
I cannot see, but I'm supposed to like it
here. I'm alone here in the light...

A crescent moon baking in the sunshine.

The stars have breathed their dust into the
souls of the heartbroken, and stitched
luminous strands together, connecting them
for eternity. I know where to find you.
Where the air is heavy and full...

And I shine there. *We shine there.*

I don't have to shield my eyes in the dark.

The ugly

Even though we see the ugly day in and day out….*I know most people are good-hearted.*

It is hard to decipher between the two, but there is a tell-tale sign. Their true intentions will come out when they are going through pain.

Watch them.

Boulders

Where does it hurt? There are days it will
hit you. A boulder upon your heart, and
try as you might you cannot lift it. Your
strength has been siphoned, and you have no
idea where it went. It was there yesterday.
But today, your mind won't move. It is stuck
on recollections from yesterday. Memories
scream loudly and render you catatonic.
You can't move. You can't breathe. The past
is heavy, and your weightlifting days are
winding down.

On days like these, *save your energy.*

Don't fight too hard. Let the memories have
their time. Just know that you will close
your eyes, *and tomorrow your strength will
be back*, and know that you *will* win days
where *you will* keep them at bay.

Home

And one day, you meet them.

Your eyes land, and they lock.
Latch on with exhausted fists of forever.
Instantly your souls shake hands
and kiss hello. And you haven't said a word.

This is what home feels like.

Secrets

My wrists are chained. Blisters rub against
a past so dark, they are a reminder that
holds my arms crossed tight. Seated—and
buttered popcorn for one. I remember the
nights during the day, and our days are
relived in my mind when the night falls.
The stage rises and the scenes I see are
remarkably award-winning. True romance
with two casting leads who have symmetrical
syncing and unparalleled chemistry. To the
world they are a match made in heaven.
The reality is that there is always another
side. A secret side that no one ever knew
about...*including me.*

Departure

Your departure was so absolute

that even when I try to recall

you and our love,

your memory *walks out the door* as well.

In the middle of everything,

you will inevitably leave.

Amble right out into the sunset,

with fog rolling behind you,

followed by a fanfare of closing credits.

And I have accepted that your exit will
always capsize your entrance into my life.

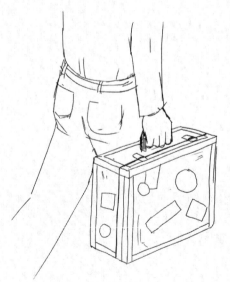

Optional

You ask for one more try.

Did she leave you, too?

Please do not insult the love I harbor for
you by telling me you finally realized
IT IS ME you want.

Am I all that is left?

Seams

I don't know how to hold on to something that was ripped from my heart. How do I hold the seams together while it beats out of my chest with each aching thought of you?

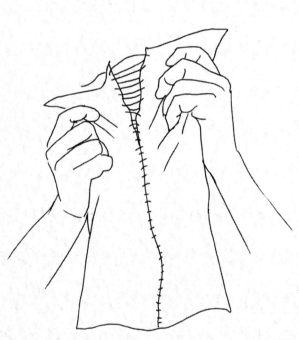

Promises

Want to make forever our home?

Love my heart today
like you promised you would yesterday.

We became one

We would lie under afghans and meld as one. You couldn't fit a sheet of paper between us because we could never get close enough. We integrated. Absorbed the other. *We became one.* He told me about his bout with depression when he was a teen. About the time he got kicked off the football team for drinking, and how he wished he had been a better son to his father before he passed away. I told him about my childhood, and about the years I went silent. I told him how it felt to want to speak but the voice wouldn't come. How I wished I could have met my dad before he passed away. I shared with him my fear of being alone

—*and he promised to never leave me.*

And years later, as I lie here and think about how freely we spoke that night...
I cannot get a word out, again. I've gone silent. The world gives, and it inevitably takes away.

My voice. My love. My heart.

Mess

How do you recover after heartache and betrayal? When you find your quivering hands holding on to a piece of cloth that you have touched countless times in the past...memories permeate the room and your thumb rubs back and forth across what *once was*. You recall yourself sitting across from a person who held the other half of your fresh heart, and you remember the way the cobalt blue shirt made his eyes shimmer against the candle on the table. You can still feel the way he looked at you at that moment, and how you envisioned both of you sitting on rocking chairs reminiscing 60 years later. You remember the countless times you washed that cotton shirt and hung it up, so it wouldn't shrink. But now the threads are tainted. Tainted by memories of the last time he wore it....You hold it now, feeling like it doesn't belong to you and it never did. Because the last time he wore it, he wasn't with you. And like always, you are left to clean up his mess.

Chances

Sometimes souls are too new to know how to
make a relationship work. They haven't gone
through a trial that broke them enough.
They haven't experienced a storm that
taught them how to rebuild. They walk away
because they think that's what you do.
We live in a society where people and
relationships are disposable—like fast food.
It's only those who have suffered a loss that
is so indescribable who are willing to take
a chance and say:

*Hey, we got this. I'm not going anywhere as
long as there is a chance the sun is going
to rise tomorrow.*

Those are the ones who have a
fighting chance.

Star gazing

I lie on my back under the full moon at night and I count the stars. I give names to all the places I have visited in my past.

I've named the twinkles in the sky: *pity, despair, heartache, lies, grief, and betrayal.*

After I separate the light from the dark in my mind, I focus on the unnamed; the destinations I long to visit one day.

Happiness, truth, self-worth, and strength.

And I make a mental note to never revisit the places I've ventured before.

Forgery

What I thought was a masterpiece,

was a counterfeit...

and I became the unknowing

recipient of a forgery of love.

Secret

Your time in the darkness will ready
your heart for the people who
belong in your light.

Remember this.

You will *feel* their love under a *secret*
glowing moon—*in your deepest moments
of despair*—not only *see* them under a full
and *public* sun.

Permanent ink

You erased the boundaries around my heart,

and circled *forever* in permanent ink.

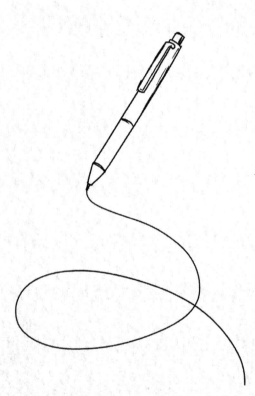

Scattered

I am bent in your direction.
I unroll my spine and stand
—taller than the saplings in the fields.
I've shrunk for so long.
A seedling you scattered.
My heart in little rows in your
funny farm.
I've forgotten my height.
My stance can dissolve lives,
but never the lies.
I dare not look back.
How did I get here?
The same place that stagnated
my growth is now setting me free.
And I feel like a bird who hears
the scream of a rusty cage door opening
a crack, and my breast beats wildly
wanting to fly free.

Good morning

On cue, my sleepy eyes adjust to
the shadows and how they run up
and down the walls;
Racing against my heart's rhythm.
Sun is dappling through,
and as always, my morning thoughts
are always of you and how I wish
I could *see you again.*
If I could describe your soul
and its effect on me,
I would say it *beckons* the addict
in me. Chanting, *"more, more."*
We're all addicted to something,
or someone in this life.
But, *my* addictions begin with the light
animating from thoughts of you,
and end with the comforting texture
of the tapestries I envision your love
is curtained behind.
I watch the draperies barely billow,
and I imagine you are saying,
"Good morning."

Surfacing

They tried to push me down.

Hold my head

beneath waves of despair.

Silencing my dreams and desires.

But, it was always *you* who tirelessly

taught me how to swim.

Winter

I wonder if she thinks of you when
the snow rains down on the meadows.
When she pulls lavender yarn
around her neck; wraps herself
in flannel and down survival wear
for the day—as you would.
I wonder if she feels you in the warmth
of her chest as she crosses her arms
against
the biting air, and inhales Winter.
When she stands against the wind,
stubborn chin tilted, imaginary force field
in place, surveying the tundra
you loved so much...
Does your memory glide through
the evergreens and reach her?
Does she think about you whilst she stands
strong in your absence, viewing what you
loved most?

Audience

I loved a man like that once.

All-consuming.

My hunger would never abate.

I breathed him in,

and he filled me.

I thought I could help him.

Help him see that he was everything.

My everything.

I wanted him to see himself through my eyes.

He was wainscoting around the rooms
of my heart. But the space was not enough

for him.

Table for two would never do.

He needed an audience.

More hands in the room to clap for him

than my meager pair.

Comatose

I don't blink when I see lightning.

I absorb its magic

Storing it for my darkest of days.

I don't jump when I hear thunder.

I mimic it when I need my soul to move.

I don't run for cover when I feel rain.

I long for it to cleanse the fear

that resides beneath my skin.

Innocence

A child's smile enamors me,
because I envy their innocence
in matters of love.

Duplicate

I wonder if I will ever love
anyone the way I loved you.
I ask myself this because I cannot
imagine my heart possessing
the capability to duplicate itself,
or to offer its contents to another soul.

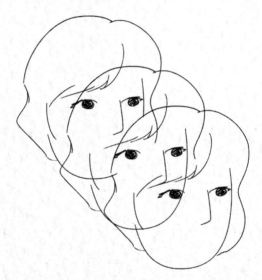

Homestead

I am criticized

for my direction.

My categorizing.

My linear headshake.

The last-minute detours

as I drag,

and I hobble.

The excursions into the unknown

my extradited soul

attempts to navigate,

in search of a homestead

that feels like home.

Flowers

Even when it was over
He gifted me with obligatory roses,
the ugliest shade of guilt.
I placed them
in the interior door
of the fridge
and slammed it shut.

No matter their giver,
I could not bring myself
to throw away something
that had been nurtured
from seed.
When someone gives you trinkets
to make up for their absence
of affection,
it makes their gift
become unappreciated.
And flowers do not deserve that.

Fragrance

I create the perfect evening
to make up for our lost time.
You give me wanton perfume
that smells like your secretary,
and I question every night
you have ever worked late.

Weight

I bend down to help with the weight,

to pick up the pieces;

Everything you've let fall throughout
your lifetime is in heaps.

The hopes, the passions, all pooling

in fountains, 'round your sides.

Nothing tangible exists as my hands

glide through the baggage.

I seek, and touch what you've felt...

But try as I might, I may never know

the person I profess to love.

I try to pick up what remains,

and I end up plunging through your depths,

on a seek-and-find mission.

I understand

You see, *I understand.*

I know we say this a lot.

You hear those magic words
and you instantly freeze.

Oh, such power one has by saying
such phrases.

I understand.

I do understand. I have been where you
have been. *Where you are.*

I've traveled the same road. Visited the
same hotels.

Overslept in arms I should have run from.

I told myself the same things you tell
yourself.

Never again.

And I vehemently meant them at the time,

Just as you did. *Just as you do.*

Yet we returned, didn't we?

Always hoping for a second chance,

a new beginning.

But, *I understand.*

Time

I know what time is worth.

It is valuable.

I have wasted too much of it in the past.

When you ask me why I spend so much of mine
being patient with you, *with us,*

I want you—*no, I need you* to see

how important you have become to my life.

Time is priceless….*But so are we.*

Curve

I need to see the shade

as it lands on the

c u r v e

of your spine

that you fear to share.

Rush

I am guilty of loving too hard,

but not hard enough

to fill your voids.

A part of me blames myself

for your indiscretions.

I go back over every argument,

wondering if my words

were venomous enough

to warrant the backlash

of evil.

Words have power.

They draw you into arms

where you do not belong.

Into circumstances

where you do not fit.

All because our hearts

long to feel the forbidden

rush of adoration.

Hourglass

We meshed like sands in an hourglass.

One grain following the other.

Landing in heaps.

Clinging in clumps,

and not knowing how we

would survive without the other.

Yet, it's possible, isn't it?

Transfer

I have an overwhelming need

to transfer the love

I feel growing in my marrow

into your patiently waiting bones.

Iridescent

You are deserving in cosmic measure,

and you have proven to the universe

that you are compiled of strength

in dependable layers

that shine bright in *iridescent wonder*.

Running

Your voice forever coasts alongside my broken spirit. Chanting, *"almost...it was almost."* I step upon uneven sidewalks, dodging the cracks I'm fearful of. Careful of my footing because my legs have ceased caring in which direction I take them. Their motivation has long since been stolen, and I force them onward now, to do my bidding. *To outrun your memory.*

Almost

I don't know when the numbness set in
completely. But it began sometime after I
found you encased in the darkness of my
quiet spaces. I knew you were still there in
spirit and hadn't left me entirely. I could
no longer touch you, and I think that's when
paralysis stole these limbs. But if I
concentrate on your shadow that sleeps
beside me, *and still tries to steal my
covers,* and if I delve *way back when—*
I can almost feel you again. *Almost.*

Eruptions

Every time you pushed me away—I still came
back. I know now that you were breaking
down my self-confidence, little by little,
trying to make me think I needed you.
Only you. You caused eruptions, and then
justified our breakups to the point where
I felt like I had to mend them in order to be
the good person.

Monster

He would tell me he was a monster, a beast.
And I should have listened, but the idea of
taming something so wild twirled the
fairytale gown in my inexperienced heart.

Warrior princess

She would tell him of her fear of dying
without leaving an impact; a remnant
of her existence.

And he would remind her of how she had
single-handedly conquered the rebellion
in his upturned heart.

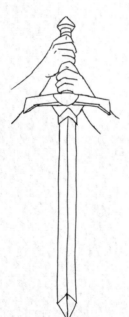

Maybe

Maybe there is a question that was never said properly.

An answer never given correctly.

An argument, that was argumented to perfection.

Maybe the conversations were never intense enough.

Maybe the secrets were not abundant enough to inspire trust.

Maybe we did everything right.

Maybe we did everything wrong.

Maybe we ran out of maybes.

Crowded soul

I want you to know that you are not what he did to you. When he hurt you, he was lashing out at everyone who came before you. You see, there were too many people in your relationship.

You, him, and *all who came before you…*

And that makes for a crowded soul.

Devour

I still have every word you ever wrote me.

Sometimes I'm so hungry for the past, I
devour every passion-laced sentence, trying
to satisfy the grieving of an empty soul.

Wreckage

It's hard trying to carve a passion-filled life out of a heartbroken soul. But you dig. You scrape the insides of the train wreck you're left with, and you find the deepest desires that reside and never left you through it all. You turn on the lights… bright. And you find the will to clean house, rebuild, and recharge. *And there will be days when you are tired of sifting through wreckage.* But eventually you organize *what matters and what does not.* You sort and compartmentalize. And you get through it.

Today

When you spend more time
loving yesterday, your heart has a difficult
time learning to love today.

Let it happen

You don't have to understand
why someone is trying to love you.
You don't have to examine yourself,
and find yourself worthy.
You just need to let it happen.
Accept it.

Insomnia

Nights can feel like years

when your heart lies awake,

replaying the moment

when it last felt at peace.

Stalled

I tried to drown myself in addictions
until I could not walk or think straight.
But all it did was push my troubles
to the sidelines and stall my heart
from moving on.

Leave

If he hurts you…leave.

If he touches you and hurts you…leave.

If he speaks to you in such a way that hurts
you…leave.

If the thought of being with him for the rest
of your life hurts you…leave.

Every second you hurt is a second of
your life

spent broken, *and you cannot get it back.*

But more importantly, it's one second

away from freedom.

Give it

If you can find it within you

to forgive.

Give it.

Give the forgiveness away.

Gift it.

It is in no way justifying the pain

they imparted.

It is not saying you deserved

the wrong done to you.

It's releasing the pain

that is ambushing

your heart.

EVENTIDE

Left behind

When does the

darkness stop calling

out to you?

At what point

do you stop talking

to the space he left behind?

You did not leave

They leave.

And you spend the rest of your life

trying to find the one that sticks

like glue.

You will stay in situations

you should not, because you think

it is your fault in some way.

Maybe it's something you have done.

If you had tried harder...

Maybe they would not have pulled away.

You will slash that whip inward,

and yet you should not.

Comfort yourself with the fact that you

tried as hard as you could.

You did not leave.

Stumble

My spirit stumbles,

drunkenly through the dark

with eyes closed,

arms outstretched,

feeling its way

heart to beating heart.

Trying to find

the one…

that reminds it

of you.

Splayed

You tell them you love them.

Thinking if you mouth the words,

the feelings will come.

You chase emotions crossing intersections,

purposely stepping on sidewalk cracks,

and climb rickety stairs.

Looking for the broken,

the ones just like you.

You think they will understand

and accept you.

But you can't fix another soul,

if your own is splayed in half.

Sword

They look at me and I feel their dismay.

I am unremarkable in their eyes and pitied.

They see the weakness and overlook

my strength.

Why is it they never remark upon my sword?

I wield its heaviness dusk to dawn.

It protects my heart at night when sleep

evades me.

I used it to cut through my sheets

in order to rise this morning.

I am unremarkable in their eyes and pitied.

And I want to scream that it is remarkable

that I am here at all.

Plain

They make you feel beautiful…

   for a time.

And when they leave,

   you feel so plain.

Pulling away

It happens in small doses.

His distance widens. Little by little.

The phone calls, the *I never want to go home* kind of nights, the consistent hand holding…eventually the kisses given *for no reason at all*, taper until your lips burn with memories.

It never happens suddenly. We tell ourselves "Here today, gone tomorrow." But he's been pulling away bit by bit for a while.

You were so busy holding on,
you forgot to notice.

Untouched

I am not untouched,

or unscathed

by this world;

even as I pretend

to be so.

I have learned

to quiet my voice,

and keep quivering lips

intact.

Lest my screams be heard

behind the shadows

of the walls I scale.

Feelings

Feelings never speak for themselves.

They depend upon you to bolster their voice.

To let them out.

To withhold is to imprison them behind the fortress you have erected out of the world's projection.

But you must find a way to let them out.

They will cling to every sinewy part of tired muscles, willing to live...trying to make you feel their power. Their presence...

Trying to make you feel anything.

Seeking

I have stood in dark places,

with arms outstretched.

Reaching for nothingness,

yet wanting *anything*.

Searching,

trying to feel the hands

of the shadows

that keep me company.

Just a brush,

a moment,

is all I need.

But even they withhold

the comfort I seek in the night.

Questioning love

We spend so much time questioning

why they have chosen us to give their love to.

We question it.

We torture the gift of it.

But we never accept their answer.

Boomerang

He will make it hard to get over him.

He keeps coming back every time you

let him go. *You throw the past into the sky*,

and like a boomerang, it comes back around,

and knocks on your front door.

Talk to me

If you want a real conversation:

Talk to me.

Not at me.

The difference lowers the barriers

of my communication skills.

Insensitive

She has been called insensitive on
occasions, because she does not seem
shocked by stories that are shared with her.
She has a habit of being blank faced.
Still. Numb. Controlled.

Maybe she is so practiced at hiding her
facial expressions that you cannot see her
heart turning over—doing flips...
nasty crying on the floor.

Pliable

It's in the quiet.
The silence is warm
to the touch.
My intuition is pliable,
elastic as I exhale,
writhing in ropes
of memories that bind
my mind and bend my heart.

Overwhelmed

You are overwhelmed and afraid of failing.

And for a moment you think of giving up,

because in your mind

that is far easier to digest

than the thought

of trying and failing

in front of your friends and family.

But don't quit. Just don't.

Breathe...and concentrate on *a reason*

that keeps you motivated.

Passion-filled life

Whether you succeed or fail trying…
They will still talk about you.
They will.
Be it good or bad.
But don't ever let another person's
opinion guide the passions implanted
in your heart.

Singing canary

You have broken a heart
that knows your secrets.
For years they ran free
in my prison yard,
guarded by my love
for you.
Now...
my heartbeats
sing like a canary.

Rewrite

Sometimes I let my life replay
before my eyes in the dark.
I go through scenes and I mentally edit.
I give the raw parts happy endings,
in my head.
A good rewrite is what most lives
need.
While it's not always possible
in reality, it does lend inspiration
for creative thinking.
Analyzing one's life is needed,
lest we forget what our personal goals
truly are.

Pedestal

I had him on a pedestal so high,

even I couldn't reach him.

Mind-bending

In every conversation we had, I felt like he was devouring every word that came out of my mouth. I had never met anyone who loved my mind more than my looks.

And that mind-bending left me spent.

Presence

When you are used to living under a towering presence—you forget your own height. It feels strange to the body when you unroll that spine and stand up straight, *giant in your strength.*

Too many years crouching, living horizontal, and growing in silence—*paused your size.* But now you touch the sky with an inner voice as tall as a grand Oak, and a heart that is weighted with motivation.

Reflection

Looking back at the weeks after. When I knew he was gone, never to return...the actual minutes of the days are blank to me now. But if I had to describe *that time in my life* with one word...it would be *Hell*.

Invisible

It was death,

over and through.

No chance of seeing each other

ever again.

Half of me died that day,

and I never got to bury that part.

I still carry the decay.

No condolences.

No flowers.

No cards.

No time off from work.

No time to grieve.

That is when I learned to wear

the mask...and get through.

Bathed in memories

I swim beneath the silvery light,

bathed in memories of my flight.

A mermaid with a soul full of years.

Scaling waves to hide the tears.

I feel more at peace

falling into the ocean,

than I ever did

falling in love.

Levy

The pain broke the levy.

And I forgot how to swim.

I didn't have the strength

to yell for help.

So I closed my eyes,

and held on to hope.

Lighthouse

She choked on the fog
and couldn't see
her future clearly.
The darkness of the past
tried its best
to take her away,
so he became her lighthouse
and showed her the way.

Soul collapse

Birthing the right
to let the past die.
I recall you...
my heart speeds up,
and the earth slows down.
My soul collapses,
exhausted from lack.
I bend down.
And birth the right
to let the past die.

Dreams come true

When you love someone,

your soul *desires*

to make their dreams

and passions come true.

Almost the truth

It was almost the truth...

the way I told him goodbye.

Like I actually meant it.

I tried to mean it.

It was almost the truth.

Owning a heart

All she wanted

was to own his heart,

but knew she would

have to gather

the pieces,

account for them

one by one,

and complete

the puzzle first.

Destination

She knew how it felt to always be the diversion,

but never the destination.

Judgment

I recant when questioned.

I defend when dishonored.

I clamor.

Nails splitting,

trying to escape

the stigma

and the judgment

of those who have hurt me.

New love

I am youth,

and eager lips.

Clingy limbs,

and raw emotions.

The onset of a love

newly found.

Caretaker

I am a caretaker
of all whom I love.
The helpless
and the hopeless.

Missing

I was missing

such a vital piece

of myself,

that when you came along

and tried to fill it....

I let you.

Fairytale

I grew up dreaming of the *fairytale*.

The one that was going to mend all

of my frayed edges, and stitch together

a *happily ever after*.

And when he came around...

He made me feel like I was the chosen one.

Martini grin

He had a martini grin.

The kind your heart orders

—shaken, not stirred,

and you feel the world spin.

Proximity

I need your light,

Your proximity.

To blind the darkness

that swathes me.

Only you have the adversity

to overshadow the bounty

of frozen heartbeats

yearning to be heard.

Where were you?

Where were you when I gazed

in wonder at an unforgiving sky?

Stars imprisoned in its space.

My North Star nowhere to be found.

Shipwrecked.

Overboard without a raft.

Suspended in air that could not hold me.

Strangling with the emotions

of being slapped around by yesterday.

Swimming towards tomorrow.

Cutting water with strokes

dripping of you.

The beginning

And it is true...

Sometimes you just want the one you love

to act the way they did in the beginning of

the relationship.

Coursing

Give me a reason.

Explain to me why my entire being

longs to trust this chemistry

coursing between you and me.

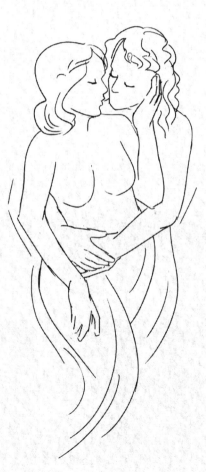

Forest

Your mind is beautiful.

A forest filled with magical wonder.

Spending time and exploring,

let me learn *to love the land.*

Birds are singing:

Let the healing begin.

Depression

I stand on uneven legs,

a bent spine and a caved ribcage,

with false bravado.

Insecurities surrounding my feet.

Toes sinking into a pond

stocked with despair and respite.

The burden becomes too much

on days like today.

I see yesterday on my left,

and tomorrow on my right.

But I am submerged in today,

and I cannot let the pond scum win.

Inhale

Lips part,

and become

wet as dew

on the banks

of a river's edge.

And I inhale the wind,

and let it fuel me.

And I am reminded

of how much

my lungs long for

the air that I withhold.

Make room

Make room for the ones who stick around
as your soul falls apart.

The ones who take your hand and say:

"I don't understand, but I don't have to.
just know, I love you."

What got lost

I may never know
what you meant to say
the night you went away.
But I heard what got lost,
and those words encouraged
me to release you
no matter the cost.

Breaking

Realize her heart is heavy,

and she treads

with a light step

to prevent it from breaking

in two.

Reservoir

You don't think you are pretty when you cry.
But nothing could be lovelier than your
sweet tears upon my shoulder, and for
allowing me to be the reservoir for all that
you have held inside.

Counterfeit

My heart has contractions.

I can feel its labor,

birthing a replica

to hang in place

of the stolen one.

Maybe its counterfeit

will be accepted

more so than

the original

that is missing.

Discard

I struggle with the phase of letting go.
How do you discard something that your
soul wears daily for warmth?

Stir

There is nary a doubt within me that I possess supernatural strength. I have held on to you to the point of *still feeling you stir* right here next to me…even though you have been gone for half of my life.

Breath holding

Your absence has been replaced by the thoughts I cling to with a bone-crushing mental ferocity.

I hold my breath, and deprive my lungs of life-saving oxygen, so I can hold your memory inside me, longer.

Thunderclap

We both made our choice many years ago, at difficult times in our lives—*when living apart was a gift to each other*. But that does not mean your memory doesn't roll across my ribs like a thunderclap. My breaths are full of memory-laden gasps, and I want you to know that *I feel every single exhalation* as I try to outrun your storm.

Locked out

Once she accepted that she would never allow him entry—*if he ever came back...* she started to live again.

I am not an enigma

Here I stand. *A survivor at living.* My soul unfolds and rises in rigid salute, paying homage to a heart that has endured unavoidable loss and the trials that each one of us will inevitably experience. I'm not an enigma. I've scoured the earth. A nomad on a quest of understanding. I've drunk of flesh until I grew numb—just so I could feel. I have sought humanity void of humility— pleading for answers to my questions.

This is *my* life. I will help a few and make a difference where I can. I do not contain the wisdom of the Universe. *I never will.* I've been searching for something lost and unfound. Yet, it has always lived within me. People, places, smoke, and counsel. Yes—they make it all bearable. *But they do not hold the answer.* They are roadblocks. Instruments of denial. The search-and-rescue mission begins and ends with you... and it is my heartfelt wish that it does not take a lifetime for you to find *what you already possess.*

Sleep never comes

It is in the darkness,

that a smoky film

hanging from the ceiling

will entice my eyes coquettishly,

and the understanding shadows

will ask for a chit-chat.

Sleep never comes, and everything
I've denied

my heart all day will resonate with
presence,

and justify their permanence to my soul.

It is in the darkness that I find the parts

of me that I have given away.

Conversations with those

I have loved and lost,

and arms that I can never fall into again,

somehow find me.

Pavement

Every time she missed a step,

knees skinned on pavement,

licking sidewalks,

and...almost giving up

She would think about how far

she had come.

And she never wanted

to go back and start all over again.

It was much easier to stand back up.

Deserving

You deserve so much more *than
what the world says you need.*

Roundtable

If we all sat around a roundtable and
shared our pasts, I wonder how similar
our tales of heartache would be?

Would we talk about the one who got away?

Hidden heart

And while her clothing shielded her heart
perfectly from public view…her armor
guarded its whereabouts *in fear of his love.*

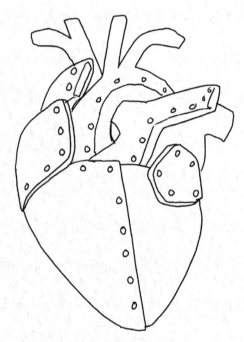

Letters

I have the letters.

The cards with the *I love you* promised

in gilded ink. I keep them as a
reminder that

some people who pass through our lives mean

their words and that words will last
a lifetime.

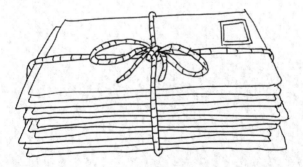

Cascading

I am a fountain.

I flow at inopportune moments.

When my words are misconstrued as bitter

in place of realization.

Cascading,

Uprising.

It clicks, and your soul is full

of reasoning. It sheds and your depth

is at my feet. Your remorse is washed away

with yesterday.

Thinking

Thinking about the one

you let get away,

while you are with

the one today,

is your soul's way

of making

your heart pay.

Prideful

I would say I am not prideful.

But how many times in my life

have I withheld words

because I did not want to be

viewed as desperate?

Immersed

With dawn I awake fitful from sleep.

I look around the room

and you are still not here.

My dreams did not bring you back.

My prayers did not unlock

the magic that would transport

you to me.

So I will have breakfast with ghosts,

and coffee with the cobwebs

of our past.

I'll drink you in with every memory.

I'll begin and end my day the same way.

Immersed in you.

Misunderstanding

I wonder how often

arguments begin

because of the

misunderstanding

of *silence.*

AURORA

For keeps

What if I told you that true love is real?

But, it remains elusive for many
of us because

hearts fear giving themselves away
for keeps.

Love yourself

Never depend on another
to love you the way
you must *first*
love yourself.
Set the bar high
—and never lower it.

Ear plugs

At some point, your soul will have to stop
believing the lies that the world shouts in
your ears and molds you to accept.

Does he

There is never an excuse or a justification as to why someone *cannot show you* they love you—if they really do.

Take note. This is the answer when you ask yourself, "Does he?"

One year from now

I have never been one of those women who need someone for one night, or been a *right now* kind of girl.

If I'm looking at you over dinner tonight, I'm trying to envision having breakfast with you, *one year from now*.

Erasure

She would lay down her life to stop others
from experiencing pain. But, if she were
granted a wish, and given the option to
erase the content of her own lifetime of
hurt and heartache—*she would pass*. She
knows it is the reason her heart beats with
such softness…now. She knows it is what
connects her to other hurting souls, and she
wants them to know they are not alone.
Never alone.

Rebuilt

She doesn't look at being broken as a bad thing. It means she has been rebuilt and transformed into the woman you have been waiting for.

Whole

I want to know why you think you aren't whole. *Who told you this?* Who told you that your soul is split down the middle—a wide expanse of barren nothingness...half full unless another being replenishes it? Who told you that you are only complete if someone comes along and stays and takes up residence next door to your self-worth? Who told you that you only contain half the amount of love that you will need to make your way through this life?

Why do you think that *half of you* resides and belongs *within someone else?*

You are perfectly complete *in your singleness.*

Just *you.*

You *are* whole.

Rain

I have stood in the rain more times
than I can count.
Trying to understand how my heart must feel
when it cries…
day in,
and
day
out.
I've lived inside this flesh for decades,
and still it does not feel like home.
I am a visitor,
an unwanted guest
causing its host to feel misplaced.

Whim

Can I ask you for...a moment?

One of those precious seconds of life
that we all release on a whim.

A fraction of your time for a
searching gaze,

a fixed stare.

Look me in the eyes if you dare.

I need to see if the man I once knew...
still dwells there.

When the rain comes

When the rain comes, *and it will,* and you are left holding on to bed sheets and goodbyes with a force of nature—remember that the storm *will pass.* Not today. Not tomorrow. *But it will.*

In the meantime, you will feel every raindrop like sandpaper upon your skin, and the winds will keep your soul leveled for a time. You will avoid the mirror because you have no answers for the questions your heart will inevitably ask. You will physically ache with sickness as the tide rolls across the buoys of heartache.

But one morning you will notice your hands shake a bit less when you are sipping your coffee. The heady scent of lavender will waft through your window and its sweetness will click with your body's need of a rejuvenating shower. *Baby steps.* You will spend more time out of bed than in it. Little things will once again bring you moments of joy, and you will hold onto these times like a lifeline. And you will never take happiness for granted again.

Something clicks

You have stored yourself in captivity long
enough. You have bagged your talents and
inner motivation like hardened seedlings.
Shoving them to live behind the walls of a
dark and cold space. Buried things have a
way of resurfacing when they are forced to
find a way to survive. Something snaps—a
change of season, and a frigid landscape
will sprout a single green stem. All the
people you have ever said goodbye to can be
felt in the shadows that you see swimming
in front of you—and behind you. Something
always comes forth from being pushed under,
especially if it has been doused in pain.

Pulse

They think I am bitter

and quite mad.

But, that would imply

I want back

what I had.

I give a pulse

to the pain

to set it free.

And I will never

a p o l o g i z e

for what you choose

to see.

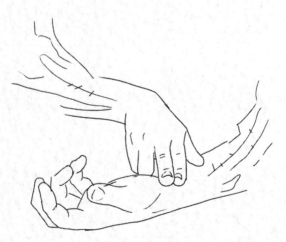

Potholes

What made you the way you are today? Was it the expectations of others that ran screaming into your space? Maybe it was the mistreatment from those you thought were sewn within your soul. The ripping makes it almost impossible to function the same way again. You have to improvise for the potholes that loss will cause. You will find yourself skipping over things intentionally in the future—because you will be terrified of falling.

Hearing voices

And I ask myself why it is that the sound of his voice is what I miss the most, when he never said what I wanted to hear anyway.

He wanted
to marry

He once confided in me his dreams of
wanting to marry. He would share it in
breathtaking detail. White-washed barn
side, elegant, rustic, and down home.
Memphis barbeque. Dancing all night as
Elvis crooned. The best man was already
handpicked, and he dreamed of a bride with
baby's breath woven in her hair. He would
tell me how pretty I would look all dressed
up in white, against an autumn background.
Between kisses he would invoke the
fairytale, and weave a future life into
tendrils of my hair. I would envision him in
a black suit and tie, holding out the only
hand I wanted to hold on to for the rest of
my life. And that image is the one I focused
on as the weeks came and went—*and he came
and went.*

He told me he wanted to marry...
only *he didn't mean* marry me.

Shine on

Some may see a wreck and destruction when
they tally her past mistakes she's made
along the way. But I see a woman who has
been tried and tested, and found *reason* to
shine today.

Gray

If a life is always a quest, asking for answers to questions, you will never really have a chance to live.

We are not meant to know the answers to everything.

There is not always a left or right, a yes or no, or a black or white to every problem.

Because I know how it feels to be *stuck in the middle, screaming "no" while feeling gray.*

Inspiration

She is an inspiration, really
—the way she gets back up
on flesh-torn knees
after each and every fall.

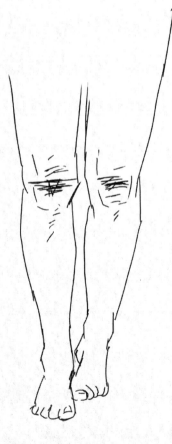

Clothe

Some days

I clothe

my scars,

and

other days

my scars

clothe me.

Abandoned

Every time I let my heart have its way,

it evacuates before the storm hits,

and leaves me to rebuild.

I am no closer

I have swum oceans to find you,

holding my breath when the waters

became troubled.

And still, I am no closer

to reaching the mainland

than when I first dove in.

Silence

Do you hear that?

That is the sound of silence

waiting for you to fill it.

I see you

Your effort is not in vain.

You think no one notices your gallant and forgiving heart—*but I do.* I see you extending kindness even when you think it will never be returned to you. You do not practice an *eye for an eye* because you do not expect to be rewarded for the depth of your heart. I see you doing the right thing, even when doing wrong would be so much easier.

I see you, and I want to say *thank you for being you.*

Moon holding

When she decided

that she wanted

to hold on to the moon,

and how it made her feel...

she knew she had

to let some people go.

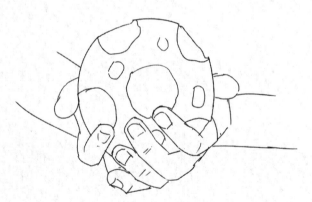

Shattered breakups

We don't always want them back when it
is over. Some breakups shatter the
rose-colored glasses you have been wearing
too long. You see exactly who they are—and
you are thankful their part in your life
has come to an end.

Regret

Are you going

to regret

walking away?

Giving up,

instead of

digging in?

Conjure

Tell me why your mind still conjures up his
memory. What magic did he use to etch his
name inside of your heart?

Miraculous life

I find miracles everywhere I look now.

A baby's toothy grin, an elderly couple holding hands, a sunset that levels you at your knees with indescribable beauty... everything is precious to me. I have experienced too many days when I could not find the will to *believe in anything*.

Captive

She was like the moon.
Held captive in the
confines of the darkness,
and glowing
in spite of it.

Devastation

It is only when the mind has suffered
devastation at the hands of pain, that it
can understand how another soul is capable
of holding it prisoner inside.

Halfway

If I know anything,

it is that I never do things halfway.

When I fall, I land on my face,

and when I break,

I shatter all over the place.

Hurt

Maybe I should have been afraid,
when I stopped seeing my own hurt,
and just saw yours.

Dangerous

There is a certain amount of *danger* in
loving someone who embraces your
uniqueness. I know it has become normal
to hide your emotional truths from the
rest of the world—out of fear.... But their
acceptance *by this daring soul* is the fire
that licks the wick of your inhibitions. And
for the first time in your life—you feel that
your difference is not a detraction, but an
attribute that makes you feel special.
Your *different* is what makes your heart
so alluring.

Forever

I wonder if we fill our hands with the temporary, because forever is too heavy for our hearts to hold.

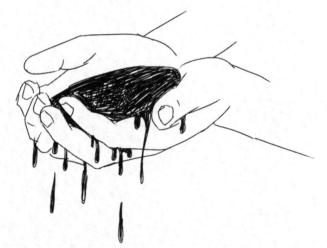

Smolder

Even if you
blow out her flame,
she will find a way
to smolder
—until she is
on fire again.

A lifetime love

It is easy to fall in love with a face in the light, but it is the ones that you ache for under a full moon that will affect you for a lifetime.

Always still there

Tell me, how many mornings will you wake
up with them on your mind? They are with
you as you brew the first cup, sitting
cross-legged in your mind like they belong
there. They're still straddling your soul
when you say your bedtime prayers. Morning
and night, holding your hand—*always still
there*. Their memory refuses to leave, even
though their legs had no problem running
out the door.

Silent heart

When you have a heart that speaks as freely as mine does, you begin to worry when it goes silent.

Healing

Healing is necessary after heartache. It is.
But be prepared for loneliness too. Heart
rebuilding is a one-man team. A crew can
never fix—what it took *one* to break. Let it
rebuild on its own.

Give it time to recuperate.

Transparent

When they talk about you, it will not always be good—or true. And most of the time you cannot do anything about it. You can't round up everyone on this world's face and brow-beat them in to loving you. But, we can *try* to be the best version of ourselves that we are capable of. *Not for others.* Never act another way to impress someone else. Do it for you. Do it because it is the best medicine for an authentic life. Not everyone will like your truth, or your kindness, or your no-nonsense way of living. It intimidates them. They are jealous of a soul who lives free to that extent. But give no apologies for living a life that is honest and transparent. There is beauty in the old saying...

"What you see, is what you get."

Forgiveness

We bandage up hurt, instead of treating it.
And I wonder why I put such stock in
temporary Band-Aids and not in forgiveness
that can last forever.

Forgiving me

I forgave you the minute you walked out the door, but the problem is I have never forgiven me...for forgiving you.

Floored

She is hard as nails,

because she had to be

to re-roof and rebuild

a few lifetimes ago.

But every once in a while,

she smiles in transparency

as she looks at him,

and he is floored

by her softness.

Rise and stand

When the hurt is fresh, there are more bad days than good ones. Prepare yourself. I got through it by throwing things. Some days I would throw my worries to the ground, and others I was catapulting myself to the floor. But with each collapse, I found it easier to pick myself back up. My body went into auto-pilot. *And that is what you have to do.* Get back up. You have been knocked down too many times in your life by those *who did not care if you fell*. Show them how beautiful you are as you rise and stand to live another day.

Mind tricks

The mind will play tricks on you. It deems someone essential to its lifeblood *after they are gone.* Your body will crave their presence more than food or water. The mind knows that you do not need this person to exist essentially, *but it likes to boss your heart around.* It has already broken the news to the poor unsuspecting thing...and it will retaliate by weeping with a pain so deafening that it will likely drive your mind insane for a time. They do this. Back and forth. No one really wins in this game of mental monopoly, but it drives the host into a frenzy of emotional chaos.

Chasing home

I chased the *idea of home* every time I left a relationship. I always felt lost, like I needed to find my way to a destination. A place where I felt at peace. But it already lived within me. I just had to open the door, sit down, and put my feet up. *Because home is wherever your heart feels at peace.* It is not a place.

It is a state of a contented mind.

Slight

She was always *underestimated*.
But even though she is slight,
she will rise and fight.

Yesterday

How many days have you wasted on yesterday? *Bow down to the past.* Thank it for helping mold you into the one-of-a-kind, fire-breathing superhero you are.

But don't long for it. Don't reach for it.

You can't go back. Think about today. Today you are creating memories and keepsakes that will become your past someday. You are going to look back, categorizing year after year, and wish you would have enjoyed this day fully and not wasted it thinking about days you can never recover. *Every day is precious in its own right.* It is a chance to leave a kind and everlasting imprint upon this Earth. *Live* every minute of every day. If you find yourself wishing you could change yesterday, then make the change today...that way when you look back with nostalgic sighs, they are for the right reasons, and you are looking back without regret.

Settling

What do you deserve? If I had to guess I would say you deserve far more than what you have settled for.

You deserve trust, yet you *accept* the lies.

You deserve respect—but you do not *demand* it.

You deserve clarity—but you have to *walk* out of the fog to find it.

You deserve happiness—yet you have never *allowed* yourself to accept it.

You deserve to be loved—but you have to remove the toxicity so that real love can come, *and stay.*

You deserve so much more than what you have settled for.

Sunshine

Sunshine rains down on me. Your words dapple upon my skin, and I shine, radiant. The length of my neck curved, burnished from a glaring warmth that is unknown to this soul. I close my eyes against the rays and as much as I want to hate the tingling on my shoulders, I cannot. You take my hand and I follow your lead. You tell me my cheeks are turning pink already. That's what happens when you spend most of your time in the darkness…. You have to acclimate your body to the light. It will take some time. A process I have agreed to. I am trying. And he is holding my hand.

Come Back

And even when I have to go away for a while
to visit the light, I promise you this...

I will always come back to find you
in the darkness.

About the Poet

Alfa would paint the world in hues of turquoise if she could. Unapologetic about her realistic take on heartache, she writes to let her readers know they are not alone in their pain. Her four children and three granddaughters, the stars of her life, were the catalysts that pushed her to force her words and her smile on the world after a lifetime of depression and anxiety. She wanted to leave something behind for them, a legacy, proof of existence, and proof that pain can be transformed into beautiful inspiration. Alfa lives in Louisville, Kentucky.

How many people have
I lost in my lifetime? I try and
recall their faces now, and as
the years move on, so do the fine
details. But sometimes…when I
am alone, swathed in the quiet
I seek, a movie reel will begin
to slide left to right, before
my eyes, and I see them, one by
one. I reach, because I have
never fully let go. I reach, so
I can find you in the darkness.

–Alfa

I Find You in the Darkness is a
book of poetry about love, loss,
and healing.

A CASTLE POINT BOOK
for St. Martin's Press

CASTLE
POINT
BOOKS 175 Fifth Avenue, New York, N.Y. 10010
PRINTED IN THE UNITED STATES OF AMERICA

castlepointbooks.com

US $15.99 / CAN $20.99
ISBN 978-1-250-20262-8

51599 >

9 781250 202628